An Everlasting Truth

Jeanette P. Hernandez

TRILOGY CHRISTIAN PUBLISHERS

TUSTIN, CA

Trilogy Christian Publishers
A Wholly Owned Subsidary of Trinity Broadcasting Network
2442 Michelle Drive
Tustin, CA 92780

An Everlasting Truth

Trilogy Christian Publishers

A Wholly Owned Subsidary of Trinity Broadcasting Network

2442 Michelle Drive

Tustin, CA 92780

For information, address Trilogy Christian Publishing

Rights Department, 2442 Michelle Drive, Tustin, CA 92780.

Trilogy Christian Publishing/ TBN and colophon are trademarks of Trinity Broadcasting Network.

For information about special discounts for bulk purchases, please contact Trilogy Christian Publishing.

Manufactured in the United States of America

10 9 8 7 6 5 4 3 2 1

Library of Congress Cataloging-in-Publication Data is available.

ISBN: 978-1-68556-175-8

ISBN: 978-1-68556-176-5

Contents

Dedication

I dedicate this book to Veritas Lux Mea, my beautiful daughter, who inspires me daily. My family that stands by me always. My Creator, for His unchanging and unending love for us all.

Preface

I came to know God, the Almighty, in a very personal way; I heard Him.

He commanded me to do something, and I did it (of course). No questions asked. I started my journey to God the moment I was conceived or perhaps even before? I always felt like I was and am on some journey with an unknown destination but filled with a particular truth that-God lives!

Acknowledgements

I want to thank my Lord and Savior Jesus Christ for my very being.

Heavenly Father for creating us all.

I want to thank all my family, (La Familia) who never ever gave up on me.

I want to thank my love Jesus Velarde, for his tireless support and endless love for me.

My daughter Veritas Lux Mea, for her great patience and kind heart.

My friends, especially Miss Cathy, my rock, who has lived alongside of me through all of my trials and tribulations.

My mom and dad, for their great example and who made me strong.

For Mrs. Debbie Cunningham, who planted a writing seed in me many years ago and has now bloomed.

For Linda who believed in me and said I could do this.

And for the entire Trilogy team and their tireless efforts to unite and empower the Christian community to spread the Good News of Christ!

Prologue

An unbelieving person, not by choice, but by fate.

Foreword

To my Dear Friend Jeanette, you will move mountains with your words.

First things first, I was not asked to write a foreword for this book. In fact, I am writing this as total surprise for my long-time friend. Since first hearing about this exciting and wonderful news that my very own friend and co-worker was in fact becoming a *published* author, I have felt drawn to write something, anything for her.

Jeanette and I have worked together for what seems like an eternity! I feel that even though we were both adults when we started, we have grown up together. We have both gone through relationships, heartache, loss of loved ones, marriage, and even having children together. They say that in most cases you spend more time with the people you work with than your own family, so in a sense, your coworkers become like family. This couldn't be truer with Jeanette. Since practically the first day I set foot in the radiology department, I knew

Jeanette was the person I had to become friends with. She was not only the "cool" the "prettiest" most "popular" kid on the playground, but she knew her stuff! She had a way of teaching that still to this day sticks with me. Her thoughts and articulations are far beyond her years, and I am constantly in awe of her mind. I was instantly drawn to her, and I have been her friend ever since.

Jeanette has a way of telling stories. She can take the simplest story like stopping at the grocery store after work and turn it in to a drama filled tele-novella, (also known as a Mexican soap opera) that always leaves you wanting more! It never failed, for years Jeanette's motto was if it wasn't for bad luck, she would have no luck at all! For many years story after story would come in, and Jeanette would just say if it has to happen to anyone, it has to happen to me! During many of these rough patches; it was hard for Jeanette to see the good side of things. Being there amongst her hard times, I would offer my support, listen, and boost her up as much as I could, but that can only sustain a person so long.

I truly started seeing a change in Jeanette when she basically hit rock bottom, and she gave it all to God. Sometimes the strongest (and most stubborn) people must hit hard before they can build themselves back up. Jeanette is one of the strongest women I know, and she has fallen many times, as you will read in this book, and although at the time she couldn't see it, God had a plan for her. Reading Jeanette's truths has truly been life changing, seeing that through all darkness a light eventually emerges, and to trust always in God. God has found a true soldier to share his word, and I couldn't be prouder of my dear friend. I am so blessed to know you and ecstatic to see where this adventure takes you, skies the limit and you deserve that and so much more!

With love always-Rox-star

The Tempest

As the Earth grew restless; there was a great rumbling about. Everything shook and tore it all apart! Their eyes looked to God and asked, "Oh Where Art Thou? Please let me see you!" And the Lord said, "Nay, I will not, for your mouths have been loosed and have been ripped asunder." I begged and pleaded. He heard my cries not. "Why must I suffer so!? Why have you forsaken me?" He answered and He said "I have not. "I never have nor will I ever. You are always in my favor. It is you have chosen not to see." I was so confused and unable to speak or think. What do I do next? How do I fix my troubled heart? "You don't," He said "I do. That was your first mistake, my daughter, you thought it was your decision and your burden to carry. I have repeatedly spoken to you. I have told you that I will take care of you, all you need to do is trust." The Earth continued to quake and rumble, and I was left all alone. I looked and I was alone. I knew not where anyone went. I was as if in a deep, thick fog. Then I saw a clearing and there before me, stood the Lord. I fell upon my face, and I cried "Please help me dearest Jesus, please fill my troubled heart with peace! I beg of you!" I pleaded with Him, but I could not look upon His face. He said to me, "You are my marvelous creation. You are my daughter. I will love you always and you are never alone." I screamed that I could not see, and He touched my eyes and removed the scales and softened my heart and I promised to do His work and I begged for His forgiveness. He said to me "It is done." The Earth continued to quake ever more, louder and stronger and shuttered and I grew so afraid! I felt as if I would be destroyed from the devastation I was witnessing and I asked "Why have I been chosen to see such horror? Have some pity on me oh Lord!" He responded and said "I will never give you more than you can handle, I will never let you be alone or suffer alone. I have been with you all your life. I will always be in your heart, and you will never suffer alone. You suffer because you are human, and you have an amazing heart. You will endure all things because I am with you." And I cried and I said, "I'm not strong enough!" He said "I never said you had to be, just trust in me! Believe and know that I will never leave you alone." Suddenly, the Earth quaked no more and all the shattering stopped, and I looked up and I saw him. He said, "Come child," and I followed Him up into the sky and I looked down upon the Earth and I knew that it would survive yet another day. That humanity would continue to scramble about and that brought me both sadness and peace. And I knew then that we did, in fact, belong to the Lord. Amen.

CHAPTER 1

Early Childhood

I was born breech. I came out upside down, as most would say. I came out defiant telling the world to kiss it. I was also a preemie. I was born in Tucson, Arizona September 10th, 1977, at approx. 8 p.m., a night baby. The nurse said I was a "great Bambina." I was to be in an incubator for months until my lungs had finally fully developed. I struggled to come into this world, and I would not allow it to just take me out.

When I was approximately four years old, my cousins, sisters and I were playing kick-the-can outside in the streets, yes, in the dark, before the streetlights came on just like everyone used to in the world back then. My cousin kicked the can so hard, it went into some shrubs, and we could no longer see it, it went behind a cement barricade and we all followed like little ducks.

To our horror, not only did we find the can, but we found something entirely different, a dead body! A man had been murdered. I can still distinctly see him in my mind as if it were yesterday; he had on gloves with the fingertips cut off, a coat and a tan beanie and he was just laying there as if asleep, but he wasn't, he was dead. His throat had been slit and I remember it still. He had what look like coffee grounds, from the dried blood, all along the length of his neck. My cousin poked at him with a stick, I'm sorry to say, and when we realized he was dead; we all screamed and went running to tell our parents.

Years later, I came to find out that the daughter of the people that we rented the apartment from, would be my future manager at Sears! She was telling the story about how one day, when she was young; a whole bunch of little kids found a body right next to the apartments her father owned. I said, "Wait on Hoff Street?" She said, "Yes!" Completely startled, looking all shocked, "How did you know?" She asked. I said, "I was one of those little kids! Synchronicity? Who knows? The universe is filled with such great mysteries.

CHAPTER 2

Generational Curses

My grandfather would tell us a story, when I was a little kid, we tell it now, to this day. It was about how our last name came to be. For those of you who are unaware last names are new in comparison to what people called themselves and or relation to their family. It was usually where they were from our whatever skill they had or job they did. The last name Hernandez originates from the Spanish conqueror Hernand De Cortez, this was shortened, to Hernandez. He was a Spanish conquistador who landed in Veracruz, Mexico and destabilized the Aztec civilization beginning in the year 1519. They conquered the land and the people who were in that land, and there was not much written history because the Spanish tried to eradicate all forms of the Aztec civilization and writing because they felt they were ungodly. Therefore, we are left with only their modified version of the truth. So, this is how my last name came to be. I am of Spanish and Aztec descent. Both of their rival blood in me, two warring parties in one body. He also told us that when he was just a child, like eleven or twelve, his father was a very rich man who had a hacienda in Guadalajara. He was a charro, a Mexican landowner, with horses that had an exceptional skill, dancing. He could make his horses dance. One night, as the story goes, he was in a bar with some Mexican police, otherwise known as federales. Apparently, some bet was made, someone lost, and shots were fired. My great grandfather killed the Mexican federale he said.

My great grandfather was always dressed like a mariachi, with real gold coins running down his trouser legs. He said that my grandpa would flick the gold coins off his sides of the trousers to the children in town when they surrounded him. I think my grandpa was a bit of an embellisher, but who knows. I guess my great grandfather became an outlaw. He said that my great grandfather hid in his own rose bushes all day outside his hacienda. Meanwhile, the federales looked for him and he fled to the "North" or "El Norte," the United States. He finally jumped on a train, disguised as a woman, and ended up somewhere in Southern California. My paternal story ends there. My grandpa was left alone with his brothers and sisters to fend for themselves, and he went to Mexico City. He was always figuring out ways to survive and a police officer would always see him. He took pity on him and took him in, and his last name was Hernandez. My abuelito's original last name was Ramirez, originally from Spain, a Castilian name. Short for son of Ramiro or Ramiro of Cortez? Who knows? He named his children each one of those two names. I read in the Bible about generational curses. It states in Jeremiah 32:18, NLT, "You show unfailing love to thousands, but you also bring the consequences of one generations sin upon the next, you are the great and powerful God, the Lord of heaven's armies." So, do generational curses follow us all our lives? Are our families truly liberated from the past?

Luke 12:5 51-53, NLT, states, "Do you think I have come to bring peace to the Earth?" "No, I have come to divide people against each other from now on families will be split apart three in favor of me and two against or two in favor and three against. Father will be divided against son and son against father. Mother against daughter and daughter against mother and mother-in-law against daughter-in-law and daughter-in-law against mother-in-law." How do we set ourselves free from generational sin?" These are the very profound questions that I would ask myself and later came to know how to be set free.

CHAPTER 3

Many Miracles

I should have known that coming into the world upside down and in the dark, would be an omen. That finding a body at four or five would pretty much define how rest of my life would go, or so I thought.

My father is a proud man. He is the most hard-working man that I have had the pleasure of knowing. He came to our great country of the United States of America with only a handful of dollars in his pocket. My mother was pregnant with me and with two of my sisters in tow and they settled in Tucson, AZ. My father taught the three of us daughters (my brother came later when I was twelve) to work hard, he treated us like boys.

We grew up cleaning yards, tending to animals, changing motors, rotating tires, cutting metal, collecting metal scraps, you name it. Whatever it took, to feed our family. When I was twelve years old, we hit an all-time low, we were really struggling. Thanksgiving was upon us, and we had absolutely nothing to eat. My dad had an old bicycle frame leaning on the side of our mobile home we used to rent, and it had been there for months. I realized it was Thanksgiving and we had no dinner plans, my mother was devastated. We were out of options. I went in solitude to my little niche of a bed that I had, and I started to pray. I didn't really know how to pray properly or follow any particular rules because we never really went to church. I knew we were Catholic, my mother taught children Bible lessons in Mexico, when she was very young, so she showed me how to say the rosary in Spanish and I could recite it all, with my eyes closed.

But I never really spoke to God or Him to me or I wasn't aware how to recognize Him. I got on my knees and began to pray. I asked the Lord for a miracle. I asked him to please help us have a Thanksgiving meal. I didn't know how or what, but I believed He could do it. If anyone could help, it was Him. I prayed and I asked. Around 4:00 p.m., someone in a white little car drove up and asked my dad if he was selling that bicycle frame that was leaning up against the trailer. My dad said "sure," extremely surprised, and the man offered my dad twenty whole dollars for an old rusty bicycle frame! We all rushed over so happy, jumping up and down and we quickly jumped into our car to go to the grocery store to buy our very own Thanksgiving dinner! We were blessed. We have always been blessed. My eyes had scales on them, and I never saw the obvious. That

God loved me! And all His children. Yes, every, single one- including you.

Anyone who is from Arizona has a monsoon story to tell. One year, we even had a NONsoon. The rains never came. It rains so sporadically here in the Sonoran Desert, that it only rains in a particular season, during the monsoon, and when it rains, it rains! It pours and it comes down and floods everything and washes spillover and dry creek beds become roaring rivers of unrelenting nature power. It creeps up on you, first a little breeze, after the rain, feels so good, smells so good, the greasewood fragrance mixed with the earthly smells is unlike anything I have ever smelled. Closest to heaven. I like to think. The air is perfect and soft and then slowly the mighty water begins to flow your way and then like a freight train it hits. It literally washes whatever is in its path miles away, taking everything and anyone in it along for one unending punishment. If you survived, then someone was looking out for you. We survived three flash floods, yes three. That is unheard of. We lived so far into the desert that our land was a flood zone. We were out putting chickens on their coops, so that they wouldn't be washed away and then we were scurrying about the three of us little girls and my mother and then the freight train sound came. My mother screamed, "Let's get out of here!" And we all ran, but it was too late, the roaring muddy waters caught us, and we all clung onto the fence for our dear lives. I remember using my elbow like a locking device lest I be let loose. My sisters did too, my mother showed us, "like this!" she yelled, and we followed her instructions. After what felt like an eternity; clinging on with our battered bodies, we just rode the tsunami of muddy water, then it ended. Just. Like. That. Afterwards, the tarantulas claimed the land. They came out by the thousands, it seemed, the whole landscape became black moving dots. Eventually, they would all disappear too. That was the first flash flood I ever survived, there would be two more to follow. One more the following year, and lastly, when I was around twelve years old. I guess I didn't know about miracles then because the very fact that we were still alive, breathing, in one piece, with absolutely no bruises, was a miracle. We had lived through three.

The desert is a punishing place. Everywhere you go, you feel as if you weren't already dead, something was trying to kill you. We had had a series of misfortunes that led us to where and how the way we lived. Most times, we had no running water, no electricity and no food. We stayed on a property where the owner allowed us to live, in exchange for us taking care of the animals. It was in the middle of nowhere. It had Saguaros as far as the eyes could see. All you could see were those crazy arms, as if reminding you that yes, there is still life out here, but we were unable to reach it.

One day, we had no water at all. We were desperate. We all got on the roof to see if the swamp cooler had any remaining water in it to drink, don't judge. My mother and us girls got on the roof, in the horizon we could see an enormous black cloud, we all cheered yay! Rain! We even had little cups with us. I was probably seven. Then it got closer, and closer still. We quickly realized that it wasn't a rain cloud at all, but a haboob, otherwise known as a wall of dirt. We headed straight to the ladder and I of course, being last and chunky, got stuck. I clung onto the ladder with my tiny hands as hard as I could, it shook violently while my mother held the ladder as I gripped the sides for my dear life! I finally made it off and we ran inside. The home we lived in was not the newest, there were holes everywhere and after the haboob hit us; a plague followed to boot. Black little bugs that came before rains, travel by the hundreds and in a gigantic cloud. We saw them too and after the haboob came through; they followed suit. They slammed into our trailer with a loud, and thunderous sound, the sound of a million pellets hitting the side of the trailer. We just crouched and closed our ears and eyes in horror! They pelted us and they fell, and they came in through the vents, tiny slits, windows, you name it. They got in. Afterwards, there were so many little black bodies that we had to sweep them out and the whole place had a stench of death. That too, was a miracle.

First, that I got to witness such an event and second, that we lived through it. Everybody wants a miracle but is unwilling to go through the lowest of lows, that it takes to get one. It doesn't come cheap and usually it is preceded by some sort of devastation. So, yeah, I am grateful for miracles. I have witnessed many and lived through many. I didn't see then what I know now to be true. That throughout all those terrible times, God protected us. He allowed us all to live one more day. Hallelujah.

CHAPTER 4

Marine Corps Daze

When I was about twelve or thirteen; my sister dated someone, whose brother was a Marine. He would drive past our place sometimes and I would see him. He looked larger than life to me. I would go to her boyfriend's house because I would babysit the younger brother and sister. I would see his picture and he looked awe-inspiring. I knew then that I wanted to be a Marine.

Around that same time, my dad told us that in the summer, we would either go to work with him and or go to volunteer. We chose to volunteer! My sister and I said our sights on the Veterans Hospital. We volunteered every summer until we were old enough to work...fifteen. We took a bus at 6:30 a.m. and went back home around 3:30 p.m. We got to eat for free! I learned to serve others at a very early age and bonus? I got to meet the very last World War One veteran in Arizona! He would ask my sister and me, if we were "donut dollies." It's a term derived from WWI, the Salvation Army sent women volunteers overseas to bring a little bit of home to the men and they would bake bread. Now I have never really been able to bake bread, but I felt great pride when he called us that. I knew that it was special. I decided then, that I wanted to work at the VA someday. I wanted to serve and help all veterans. I felt it was an honor. I work there now, to this day. It is a privilege to serve those who have sacrificed so much.

I worked incredibly hard in high school, paid my dues, lived on our own with my sisters. We grew up fast. We paid our own bills, bought our own cars and mom and dad guided us and we basically became full-fledged adults at sixteen. We had all the full responsibilities that adults do now. I had a job, my entire high school career and so did my sister. I was a mentor, a tutor, Treasurer of the Honor Society. I played tennis. I learned German, I was an Academic Decathlon, and an Honor Roll student. I even took swimming because I did not know how to swim, and I knew I needed to know to be a Marine. So, I made sure I became proficient, and I did. Combat survival swimming is essential for a Marine. I graduated in 1996 from Cholla High School and I was ready to leave Tucson. I remember my dad saying that we had to give back to the country that had given us such great opportunity. I am first born generation. I am first Marine in my family. I am first in graduating college. I am very proud of my Mexican heritage and American upbringing. I did not yet realize how much I needed God. Oh, but did I learn! I learned quick and in a hurry. Amazing how quickly I became religious in the Marine Corps. Boot camp was seriously difficult. I ended up in Parris Island, Marine Corps Recruit Depot, in South Carolina, in the very hot summer in June 1996. I would go through four months of physical and mental punishment.

They basically destroyed the old me and built me right back up like forged steel. I was but a memory of my former self. I quickly realized that the world did not revolve around me and or my needs, but that I had a greater purpose to serve others. My life had been leading up to that same message all my life. I found myself going to church every single Sunday. I prayed that I would somehow survive and come out a Marine. I never really felt like God left me, however, I felt like I revered Him like a great uncle, a separated person. As if not really part of my family. I am ashamed that I felt like that at some point in my life. I realize now that it was the adversary, whispering in my mind that God was this majestic man that couldn't be bothered with a peon like me. Had I known the truth then, how many heartaches could I have prevented?

Somehow, some way, I pushed through. I pushed my body and my mind harder than I ever thought was possible. I learned that I could do things most people only dream of doing. And I learned many skills in the Marines. I accomplished tasks and learned things others only dream of doing. I became a marksman shooter. They called me "Dead Eye." I knew that whatever I wanted to do, I could. All I needed was dedication, and hard work; something I had been very familiar with. I graduated September 1996 and went on to my new duty station. Camp Johnson, North Carolina. I was to go to Personnel Clerk School. I was to basically become a pencil pusher at my nearest reserve unit back home. That did not happen right away. Right before discharge, so that I could go back home, go to school, use my scholarship and be a weekend warrior, they found a tumor.

I had developed a baseball sized solid mass in my abdomen. It had obliterated my ovary, fallopian tube, and had enervated itself into my endometrial walls of my abdomen, very close to my spine. Needless to say; I didn't get to go home anytime soon. I had dreamt of going to the University of Arizona, the ROTC program and become a doctor. I had my whole life planned. I busted my butt in high school, achieved many things to get to my so-called perfect life, and now, here I was, with a tumor and no real knowledge if I would be able to ever get home.

Once the tumor was discovered; I was permanently stationed. The doctor who discovered it, saved my life.

She said, I was lucky to be alive and that it hadn't busted. I would have bled to death. Comforting thanks.

I was nineteen years old. I had no real-world knowledge of anything really. I was all alone, I may as well have been on the other side of the moon, like the dark side. I was made to stay in the hospital so that they could monitor me until my surgery. The tumor was finally removed in December of 1996. No one visited me except the company commander who had pity on me. I am grateful for her. Those months are blurred. I either chose to forget or they are so painful that I cannot bring myself to recall them. I walked around in a daze. I had prepared all my life to defend my country and planned my whole life and now who would defend me? I lost my sight. I lost my way. Everything I knew, everything I had worked towards, was gone, in one swift diagnosis.

My entire life had imploded itself upon me. It hurt. It hurt in a manner that is inconceivable to many. I had worked, since I was twelve, to do everything necessary to become what I thought was successful, so that I did not struggle the way I had since I was a child. And now, I had no clue what would happen next. I languished and I grew angry, and resentful. I was very distraught. No one knew my pain, God did, but I was unaware of His presence. I ended up having a fifteen-hour surgery. I became a case study. An entire team came from Bethesda to evaluate me, and I was treated like a celebrity of my own little crazy show. After months of therapy; and recuperating and three more subsequent surgeries; I was allowed to finally go home.

I never did become a reservist. They activated me. And I was all alone in North Carolina. Stick country, I used to call it. I had no family, no clear sight, no Mexican food, no real job, no clarity. They tried to keep me busy and help me, but I was not doing well at all. I became despondent and I was surviving all alone in what felt like a foreign land. My health continued to decline, I was eventually sent home on humanitarian reasons, and I needed more medical attention. I was stationed eventually at a duty station called Bulk Fuel Company Alpha in Tucson. They made a spot for me, so that I could heal and get better. I became part of a dozen active-duty Marines who take care of local reservists, about three hundred of them. I became a VA patient in 1999. I developed endometriosis, debilitating scar tissue that grows rampant and never really goes away and or stops growing. I was eventually medically, honorably discharged, with no hope of ever having children. They said I was rendered infertile. I felt a piece of me die when I was told that.

All my life, I pictured this perfect scenario in my mind, I would graduate with Honors, become a Marine, serve my country, become a doctor, save someone and get married and have a family. Life would be perfect, and I would never, ever suffer again. That was my life model. I would do that. Only me. God humbles, and He humbles hard. My entire world crumbled and now I was discharged, no job, no scholarship, no money, no career, no clarity, no peace and now, to add insult to injury, not even ability to even become a mother. I screamed at God. "Why do you hate me so much?! What did I do to deserve this???!!! Why did you do this to me???!!! What did I ever do???!"

I had done everything, and I mean everything right, and still, it wasn't enough, and it was all taken away from me. The scales on my eyes grew heavier and thicker.

CHAPTER 5

Midlife Crisis

I call my early twenties my midlife crisis because by then, I felt like I had lived a hundred years. The pain and suffering of all my life had finally caught up with me. I had two jobs, two mortgages, car payment, and I was barely hanging on. I had been with my then partner Eric, since graduation. We moved in together, bought a home, started a business. I was going to school to become an X-ray tech. I had been given a second chance at school through a veteran program called Vocational Rehabilitation. They basically provided me with a new opportunity, and I was now officially a disabled vet at the ripe old age of twenty-two. It took me five years to get through school.

The years went by, I no longer felt or heard or knew the Lord. I was spiritually empty. Physically broken, and mentally blocked. I was not living, I was surviving. I was barely staying afloat. We were okay for a while and then things started to go downhill fast. Eric and I had barely been making ends meet. I had two jobs and went to school full time. I finally graduated from college at twenty-seven. I felt old. I felt helpless and I couldn't believe I was going to graduate. I was living on fumes. I had survived, I managed to graduate college. At any moment though, I felt as if something horrible would happen, that a plane would fall out of the sky and of course, why not, land on my head and squash me. That is how I felt most of the time. As if at any moment; my life would leave me. I had no anchor, no substance, nothing really, that was mine, if only my mind. Even that was questionable. I became a war machine. I went into survival mode, and I stayed there for many years, until my life was really, again threatened. Not by a flood, haboob, plague, lack of food or water, nor a tumor but a real-life demon. An intruder high on drugs.

It was December 2007 and Eric, and I were sleeping and at home around 3:00 a.m. I had a brand-new Dodge Charger that I had gifted myself for all my hard work! My hard work had finally paid off. I had a really good job as an X-ray tech, and I got to serve our veterans. I was not about to let this guy who was whacked out on drugs, take my car. We heard what sounded like the engine, trying to turn on and Eric jumped out of bed, grabbed a shotgun and went outside to see what was happening. We weren't sure what was happening. I stayed in bed, and I didn't think to get up. Somehow, I fell into a deep sleep and then I woke up at the crack of a gunshot. I jumped out of bed, and I ran into the laundry room which was also the entrance to the back door. To my absolute horror, I see that the guy had Eric in a weird wrestle move, choking him, and they were wrestling for the shotgun on the ground outside. I could not believe what I was witnessing. I started screaming and I yelled at the guy to let Eric go and he said to Eric, "Hand her the gun and I won't hurt you." I yelled "For God sakes! I will give you my car just let him go!" And they were still wrestling. He yells again for him to give me the gun, I guess he didn't realize he had made a huge mistake. I take the shotgun from Eric's hands, and I started to walk up the stairs as slowly as I could trying not to make any sudden movements. Unfortunately, he still had a handgun pointed at Eric. Eric somehow runs into the washroom, I'm standing there with the shotgun, he grabs it, by the time we turn around, the guy is on us, and he was once again physically touching Eric's head with a handgun. I saw that on the floor, there was a tire iron and I grabbed it instinctively. Now, all three of us are wrestling with the shotgun together because he still had a hand on that too and he was so high, I felt like he had Superman powers. His strength was beyond belief. Now, it is at this time when time stood still. I looked into the intruder's eyes, and I knew then that he was filled with a real-life demon. Believe it or not, I knew. His eyes were completely black, and he was gritting his teeth. I remember pleading with him to take the car and please put the gun down.

I realized there was no negotiating with him. That he was passed rationalization. All my patient care skills and taking care of the sick, was almost crippling me. I could not bring myself to hurt him and that's when I heard Eric yell at me and he snapped me out of it saying, "Hit him!" and I snapped out of it and my Marine kicked in and I remember saying, in my mind, "Someone is going to die tonight, and it is not going to be us!" So, I grabbed that iron, And I start wailing him on the head as hard as I could. He started to lose his strength and consciousness and loosened his grip on the shotgun, and we still had the shotgun in our hands, and we straightened it out and pulled the trigger. He spun around ran and away! He leaped and bounded away like a gazelle and all that was left was a blood trail. The police showed up and canines, and they go looking for him. I was read my Miranda rights and we were separated. A detective showed up, we are interviewed. I was put in the back of a police car, and I thought I could be arrested tonight and go to jail for trying to save my own life! I was sick to my stomach. In a blink of an eye, my whole life changed. We had to leave the house. Something happened that night. Somehow my strength left me. I could no longer work at the pace I had been working for so long. I had worked so hard, for so many years that I simply could not do it anymore. I had reached my breaking point. The intruder was found days later by dumpster and bleeding out. He was eventually charged and served ten years in prison. I eventually forgave him in my own mind and myself for shooting him. It was not on purpose that he was left alive, but I am grateful that he didn't die and then I did not kill someone. That was the beginning of the end, we lost everything.

CHAPTER 6

Reckoning

I had been working all my life it felt like I had worked so long and so hard that it felt like I was going full throttle for over fifteen years. Morning, noon and night, my days were filled with work. I had been given an immense opportunity and I felt lucky to work at the veteran's hospital to see such amazing people who had served our great country. I was very proud of that. However, I wasn't making ends meet. I had also been helping Eric in our business for almost twelve years and when the incident happened, we had been only breaking even. And in that last year; we finally came up short. I was going to school to get my second degree full time and I would also help my parents clean at their cleaning business for extra money. I also freelanced as a makeup artist for Christian Dior part time. That was one of my most favorite things to do.

I finally broke. Something snapped inside of me. I felt broken and unable to put myself back together. I couldn't keep up with two mortgages, car payments, shop payments. We lost our house, kept the rental. We lost the shop. We lost his car and we moved. We were absolutely lost. We moved to our rental and had to fix it. We moved in. It had been so used and destroyed that nothing in the house was salvageable. Years of tenants using it showed and we needed to remodel it. We left our old home with only a tiny truck full of stuff. That was it. A mattress, a lazy chair, and a Bible. That is what I had to show for working all my life, and this gutted house by my tireless efforts of working 24/7 since I was fifteen years old. Not a very good investment. Oh, and this Bible. Which, I didn't even buy. A customer I had once at the Chanel counter, at Dillard's (one of my many jobs), had so freely given to me. We slept on the floor on the mattress. Yes, that was my life. Lying in the middle of the living room, that was my reality.

I was so completely and utterly lost. I had been given the hardest knocks of life that I did not think that it was possible for me to ever fully really wake up from my living nightmare. We were in debt. We had nothing left and we were but a former shadow of ourselves and nothing to show for our years of hard work and dedication. I kept trying to move my life into this picturesque, happy life that I thought I needed to be happy. I would say "When I do this, I will be happy. When I do that, I will be okay and when I do this, that will happen. When I complete school, I will be fulfilled." I never stopped to thank God and or acknowledge Him or ask Him to liberate me from my living nightmare because I honestly didn't know I could! How stupid is that? I just took a deep breath and pushed through that is what I was raised and trained to do. Just keep going and surviving. The Bible kept us company. We started reading out of boredom really, we didn't even have a television. I had driven away from our old home and left everything in it. I was simply too tired to care. I was eventually diagnosed with severe depression and PTSD. I also suffered from debilitating panic attacks that would crush me from the inside out. I could not pull myself back together.

We began reading the Bible and discovering its riches and messages and it started to bring a flicker of life back into us. We were reading every night for almost two months, nothing in particular, just random passages and we would flip through the Bible and chose but that was all we needed. Eric suggested we join a church. I hemmed and hawed and said "Okay," and then he says, "But there are so many, how will we choose?" The Book of James states very specifically and answered our prayers. James 1:5, NLT, states, "If you need wisdom, ask our generous God, and he will give it to you. He will not rebuke you for asking."

We had hit rock bottom. There was nothing left. We had no money, no real home, just an empty shell of a house. We had no furniture, no refrigerator, no TV, nothing. We had a little cooler for eggs and milk. I still had my job and my car. That was it. At least we had that. We had a Bible. We got to that James verse, and we did just that. We got on our knees and prayed. What could we possibly lose? We had tried our hardest and worked like maniacs and yet still, had no real thing to show for it. No real return on our countless hours of work and school and sleepless nights. We were lost, felt empty and broken. Life had officially kicked our butts and we were defeated. What could we possibly lose that we hadn't already by simply just praying? Desperation is a great motivator.

I always felt like I was an inch away from going under. I always felt as if any minute I would somehow float away like I did in those floods as a child. That the Earth meant nothing, that it couldn't even sustain us, nothing made any sense to me. Not life, not my job, my relationship. My role in the world. Not even my reason for being. I began to question everything. My very own sanity was in question. I had always been so sure, so convinced, that I could do anything I wanted to, that I could mold my life into perfection and yet here I was begging on my knees to God, the universe, anyone to take pity on me and hear my prayers in this empty house. That moment was a defining one. It was one of the lowest points of my life. Or it was one of my highest? I even wondered, why am I even alive? What is the point of all this madness? Just sadness and working as if one were in a hamster wheel and for what? To end up worse than before? Something had to give. I believe deep, somewhere buried very deep, that there was a tiny flicker of life left in me and I began to pray. We prayed hard. We prayed earnestly. We prayed until the sun came up, on our knees.

I asked God for guidance that night. I asked Him to direct me to the church that he wanted me to attend to so that I would not feel so lost. I asked for clarity and discernment. I begged Him to see what I had failed to see for years. I had tried my hand at life and had failed miserably. Life had handed it to me. No one can say that what I did, I didn't do great. I had failed epically. If anyone could fail and fail good, it was me. I blamed everyone for my problems and failed to see that all I had to do was look in the mirror and see plainly that the reason I was sitting in all that misery was a consequence of all the choices I had made in my life. Those were my results, no one else. I had put myself there. I was angry. I was resentful. I wanted to be angry. I walked around angry and hurt. The world had treated me badly. I didn't choose my circumstance it had happened to me?! In all that solitude and emptiness, I pondered about my life. I wondered about how my life had turned out, why and how I had lived and asked myself what have I done to contribute to myself and my family?

I began to think about what my whole life had been like. I started to think that maybe my life had been a mistake. Maybe I didn't belong here? Maybe I had been an accident? Why did I feel that way? I only knew that I thought it was true. Somewhere along the path of my life, I had lost my way. I used to read the Bible as a young girl, but I stopped when I was probably around fourteen. I saw how people struggled to live, I saw how my family struggled and I pondered what my purpose was. Why were we even put here? Why were we? Who were we? What was in store for us all?

The truth of the matter was that I was too blind to see what was plain as day. That I was *ALIVE* and that should have been enough. That my very life had been a gift. The fact that I woke up every single day was a gift. My struggles were my gift to the world. It made me, shaped and molded me. Through a process of fire, I became who I am. I had even failed to see that, as well.

CHAPTER 7

The Great Awakening

The very next morning, after our earnest prayer, I went about my usual way. It was a Saturday and I had planned a sales party on behalf of my brother for all my coworkers at my sister's house. In the middle of all my displaying and fixing; the doorbell rang, and my sister yelled saying "J it's for you, answer the door!" I went and opened the door. To my immense surprise, two bright eyed, young missionaries are standing there with their ties and name tags, and I was perplexed. I said almost without realizing it, "How did you know I was here?" Wait, what is happening here?

I invited them in, and they were cordial and walked in and they said they felt compelled to stop by and say hello. I asked my sister if she had invited the missionaries over and she asked, "What missionaries??" I said, "Them!" She said, "No?!" And we giggled like children. I was bewildered because I had prayed where to go and here, they were. They said "Well, we can see you're having a party." And they gave me a *Book of Mormon*. And they left as quickly and quietly as they had arrived. My sister lives in the middle of nowhere. I often wonder how those young men found their way to us anyway. I guess they had GPS. God piloted system. Eric called me about one hour later with some exciting news. He told me that he went to pay for something, and an LDS card, a Latter-Day Saint card with a missionary's name flew out of his wallet along with all his cards and old receipts. He said it's an LDS church! He was excited. I proceeded to tell him my story too and he called the number, and they gave him the name of the missionaries in our area. Eric began meeting with them on a regular basis, me not so much.

We had agreed to be open minded and did not have any preconceived notions or prejudices towards any religion and we agreed that whatever church approached us first, that was where the Lord wanted us to be. The two young men that walked into our humble house were a gift. They were one of the finest young men we had ever met. They were kind, gracious, polite, and stood in truth. We felt we were in God's presence when they were around. They even made the house smell like fresh baked sweet bread! Eric loved them instantly. I had my reservations because, of course, I always knew best. They taught us about the gospel, the good news of the Lord. They taught us about the plan of salvation, and all about Jesus Christ and His days of ministry and His life on Earth. Eric knew right away that he wanted to be baptized, no doubt about it. Me, again, not so much. Then they asked us something altogether different. They asked us if we would consider getting married? Huh? Eric and I had been together almost fifteen years by then and had considered it but never got around to doing it. We decided to do it. And we decided we wanted to get baptized. They set the date for August 6th, 2011. I, on the other hand, still had my reservations.

I was, to put it plainly, very afraid. I didn't really want to do it, get baptized, that is. I didn't really agree with some of the things being taught. I was being very stubborn. I was afraid of letting go. I wanted to do what I wanted to do and not give in to the Lord. That is what I was truly, deeply afraid of. I thought I was going to be forsaken, but I was already removed from the Lord! I had stopped growing spiritually and I didn't even know it. I was lost. So lost in fact, that I didn't even know that I was lost! One of the elders suggested that I pray. To pray what I heard was true, if the gospel was true, to ask heavenly Father if the church was true, and if this was the right thing for me to do. So, I did. I got on my knees, and I prayed. I prayed with my whole being, my whole heart. I woke up the next day and was unable to recall any dream. I had not received a sign. I went about my day.

I went to drop Eric off and as soon as he exited the car, I began to contemplate. I began to wonder if the church was true. What it all meant for me, and I was basically talking to myself. I was trying to solve life's great mysteries like I always did. Or so I thought. I was deep in thought and talking to myself, then right before I drove out onto direct traffic, I heard a voice. I heard it as clear as day. I heard him speak to me and he said the following, "Go and be baptized, for this I command, and I AM the Lord." I was in complete and utter shock! I was in complete disbelief! My whole body, my very being, felt like it was on fire. I was shaken to my very core. I felt like I was reverberating. The air felt electric and there was a buzzing sound and I felt like I had been hit by lightning and was literally thunderstruck. I could not believe what I had just so clearly heard. So, I thought "What in the world? I must be imagining things!" I even looked in the backseat and the rearview mirror to make sure no one was hiding back there! I then became fully aware that it was in fact, the Lord himself speaking to me. Before my initial shock was even over, he continued to speak to me. He said "You have been given many special gifts, yet you continue to waste them. You have known the truth all along, yet you continue to doubt! Why?"

I just broke down crying, saying, "I don't know, I am afraid." I realized then that I had been afraid my whole life. I was afraid of giving into the Lord and allow His blessings to enter my life in exchange for my promise, to do His will and not my own. I knew that His existence was real. That I was alive because He allowed me to be alive. That He was in charge, not me. I had been trying to mold my life, my own life, and had not been very successful, I might add, and I was being stubborn. I was afraid of letting go of my ego, my selfish ways. I knew I needed to do His will! To let go and let God!

I knew then, instantly, that I had been wrong my entire life. I had finally admitted it to myself. No one wants to hear the truth, not really because it is scary! I was crying and I was scared and so ashamed of myself. I was ashamed of my stubbornness. My absolute refusal to give up my ways and I finally said "I am sorry! I have been afraid." He said, "Fear not, now go and be baptized, for this I command, and I AM the Lord."

Then it stopped, it all got quiet. I realized I was still sitting in the middle of the road. I backed into the parking lot, and I was hysterical! I was shaking. I couldn't pull myself together. I called Eric and told him what had just happened, and he told the elders. When I got home from work that day, I told him that I too, wanted to be baptized. I know that what I heard was absolutely, without a doubt, real and audible. I felt it and I heard it with my whole being. I will never forget it, as long as I live. I will never stop thanking Him for having graced me with His presence. I am truly grateful and humbled by the whole experience.

The day I was baptized was life altering. All my family and friends were there. They were all very supportive and we were married.

When I was submerged in that baptismal font something incredible happened. All the pain, anxiety, despair, heart breaks and body aches and suffering that I had been carrying with me, all of my life, went away! Just. Like. That. All of it. And all I had to do in exchange was to trust in the Lord?! Why hadn't anyone ever told me? All that suffering, all that pain, for no reason, other than that I had caused it to myself. I had no one else to blame!

When I came up out of that water, I felt as if weight, real physical weight, had been lifted out of my body. That it had been taken, washed and or lifted away by the Lord himself and it was awe-inspiring! An indescribable feeling of happiness, peace and contentment spread all over me and filled me with new life. I felt all bright and new, like a brand new, shiny penny! I felt alive!

I had been given a second chance. I knew He had grace sufficient enough for me. That the Lord graced me with his presence and gifts. The old me died that day and when I took that breath in, I was born anew. I was literally reborn. My whole life changed in that instant and I became a brand, new, person. I became a spiritual person. I had shed my old self.

CHAPTER 8

The Dream

"Walking on water with Jesus"

I woke up and I was on the beach. I felt the cold breeze in the air, and I smelled the salt spray in the air. The ocean was a clear aquamarine blue. I shielded my eyes from the sun, and I looked towards the ocean. Sea gulls were circling above I saw the water lapping below my feet, cold, wet, and sandy. As I went into the ocean, a little further, I saw a figure. The figure was far away in the middle of the water and on the surface. It was Jesus! I dropped to my knees and wept. There was Jesus! "My Lord!" I cried out. I put my head in the sand and wept some more. The salt burned my eyes, and my tears cleared the pain. "Jesus!" I cried out, as I stood up and looked, He beckoned me, and I went forward on top of the surface! I began to run fast and then faster and I was laughing, and I said, "Don't leave! Wait for me!" He smiled and when I reached Him I was almost breathless, and I couldn't console my crying. My chest was heaving and hurting, my heart ached as I felt the love, He felt for me. It was far too much for me to bear. I simply wept and He asked, "Why are you weeping?" I said "I don't know. I love you so much and I am afraid I am not worthy for you to love me back." And He responded and He spoke. "I have loved you since all of eternity. You and everyone else." And He smiled. I smiled back at Him as the tears streamed down my face.

There we were, in the middle of this glittering ocean, on the top of the surface as seagulls circled above. I looked far off into the distance, and I saw the most beautiful cliffs I have ever seen. The tops were endless, and they were covered by clouds and covered in shade. "Wow!" I exclaimed "Look at that!" I said excitedly and I was smiling ear to ear and Jesus laughed at my wonderment and I asked Him randomly "Why did you make me forget?" And I began to weep again, and He said, "It was part of your spiritual growth. You had to choose me all by yourself and you did." He spoke. "I love you so much, I died on Earth for you and all of mankind so that you could enter into my Father's Kingdom, and I walked as you did, and I felt as you do now." I dropped to my knees on top of that deep, blue ocean and I said "I am so sorry, I did not know for a long time, please forgive me, I am so ashamed. And He said, "I have forgiven you, please arise." I did, and He took my hand and He said, "Look!" and I looked, and I saw above magnificent clouds start to form with the most beautiful light that I have ever seen. It began to form right before my eyes and I saw it grow in immensity and I grew in amazement and then I saw a tunnel began to emerge and I heard singing, thousands of beautiful voices or wavelengths or sounds unlike any that I have ever heard. The sound engulfed Jesus and I and my whole being.

I was overwhelmed by the sound, and I knew they were Angels singing. They were praising the Lord and I was in awe, and my eyes, I felt as if my eyes would leave me in such beauty. I had to catch my breath and suddenly I realized I had no lungs, no breath, no eyes and yet I saw and felt and breathed like I never had before. I was a particle; a beam of light and I was everywhere and with all the angels and Jesus. Then I looked down and I was restored in a white cloak with my celestial body, and I had been welcomed into the gates of heaven I was so happy and I thought of my wonderful family and I asked Jesus, "Where are they?" and He said "Some of them are here but you are the first to acknowledge where you are and whom you have chosen to serve." And He asked if I wanted to serve humanity and help them, and I didn't know for a split second and I then said, "I want everyone to know about you and what this place holds and the universe." He then asked, "How will you choose?" I answered, "How do I know what you want me to do?" "Thy will be done." He said, "You only have a small amount of time to bring others to this truth. What do you want to do?" I said in agony, "I don't want to leave you, dear Jesus, my Lord, please don't ever let me leave your side again!" I cried out and he said, "I have never and will never leave you." And then I slept. I fell into a deep sleep, and I woke up again. I knew I only had a short time to get everyone baptized. The dead, the ones who are dead in spirit and I knew what I needed to do. My mission had finally been revealed to me. Please heed my warning. Those that are not baptized will not be allowed to enter the Kingdom of God. Heavenly father has given us all an ample opportunity to choose before it's too late. I love you all very much. I want us to all move forward in spirit, commit to be united. One Humanity. One mankind. Forever.

CHAPTER 9

My Miracle

I got to tell you something, the adversary, he is cunning. He had me fooled for many years. I know that God lives. I see him every time I look into my beautiful daughter's eyes. I know because she lives. I was told time after time that I was infertile. That I would never have children and I believed it. Eric and I had been together a long time and married only two years and my biological clock was ticking. I was thirty-five. I needed to know, for sure, if I could indeed bear children or not. I had been seeing the same OBGYN for sixteen years! She assured me that I could not. I believed it. And after many years of deception, I had a conversation with God.

We began attending church regularly. I was selected to be a primary school teacher. I was to teach eight-year-olds all about the Bible. I accepted my assignment, with some trepidation, and I went with my newfound knowledge of God. I saw their bright little faces every Sunday, I taught them for almost two entire years, and it broke me and left my heart in pieces every single time

I taught them. I remember asking the Bishop why he
had chosen me to teach their children. He responded
very wisely that perhaps it was them, that were sup-
posed to teach me. I was very perplexed. I took my assignment, nonetheless. It was the best thing I ever did.
They taught me patience. They taught me reverence.
They taught me diversity. They taught me humility and
they filled my heart with laughter and wisdom. I am
forever grateful. My breaking point was, however, one
Mother's Day. All the mother's got a flower. I got one too
and I felt instantly like an impostor. As if I merited it. I
felt like I did not deserve it. That I was simply an impostor acting as if I had a child.

I walked away quietly into the classroom, with
flower in hand, and I just cried. I just broke down and
cried in front of the children. At this point, I was in the
middle of a divorce and working to fix my home every
minute I had and teaching the children on Sundays. I
was doing everything I could to ease my thoughts in my
head. "Get out of your head, it's a dangerous place." So,
I worked in replacement of thinking. But this day, this
day, it was simply too much for me. Instead of teaching
them, I just cried. I am ashamed to say that I had a weak
moment, and I broke down crying, right in front of my
little audience of eight-year-olds. One of them asked
me "Why are you sad?" and I blurted out barely audible,
"I'm lonely," then he asked me again "Why are you so

lonely?" I said, "Because I don't have my own family," I answered sheepishly. I looked at them and I saw their little faces looking at me with such pity and horror as if I had three heads and he continued "Why don't you have a family?" He was genuinely concerned, and I said, "I don't know." And I cried. I just let it all out and those beautiful little angels just surrounded me and looked at me as if I were a wounded animal and they looked at me with such sadness and pity.

They were wise beyond their years, and they comforted me. And I felt very inadequate. I never taught again. I just could not bring myself to face them or my ugly truth that I couldn't bear to see their little faces again and that none of them belonged to me. It hurt me to see them. To see they belonged to others with their own families. I was once again lost and broken. I had lost my marriage. I was injured at work and now I was thirty-six and in the middle of a divorce with no children to call my own. All I had left was my faith. To add insult to more injury, I had finally gotten approval for in vitro fertilization that March by the VA, after all those years, I finally had gotten the opportunity to possibly get pregnant and now no one to have a child with. I had been waiting for approval for months. And now, it was too late. So, one day, after the church incident, I finally decided to have a talk with God. I poured my heart out, I cried, and I said "Lord if you don't want me to be a mommy, I guess I won't be. I will be the best auntie I could be, and I will never again ask you why I don't have children ever again, or my very own family, just bring me peace." And I apologized for questioning Him all those years. Always with the questions. I wrote a letter, and I poured my heart out. I wrote Him. My own very private letter to God and I put it away.

Three weeks later, my old high school sweetheart found me through social media, and we reconnected. We renewed our relationships and became a couple. By the following Valentine's Day of the next year, I was officially pregnant! Naturally. After two ultrasounds to verify it was, in fact, a real pregnancy. I saw my beautiful baby on that ultrasound only weeks old and I promise you, I saw a spark! She is my miracle. Her very birth was nothing short of miraculous. She was born without a pulse and or breathing and yet the Lord filled her life with breath only moments later and I was granted my greatest wish to be a Mama. To be given a great task to take care of another human being. I was extended the greatest blessing of all, for me, motherhood. Just when I had given up on all hope, the Lord shone his great mercy upon me yet again, and I now have my very own family. Even though I only have one child, it is Jesus Christ and Heavenly Father who made her possible. I thank God for her each and every single day. She is my greatest miracle. My little earthly Angel.

I often think about that day, with the children. How they were so innocent and genuinely interested in me and my situation. They had pure hearts. They were all just pure truth. I love them all. I love them still. I guess I did have more children, I was just too dumb to see that too. I will never take the Lord's gifts for granted again. Now, they are all grown up. I wonder if any of them remember me and my Bible teachings? I hope I taught them even a quarter of what they taught me. I pray I never lose sight again.

CHAPTER 10

The Crucible, A Pandemic

Finally, my life was starting to take shape. I have a family of my very own, my home is finally repaired, and I am now earning enough to be okay. That's when I thought, everything would finally be normal, the pandemic hit. COVID-19 happened. A pestilence was thrust upon us.

Sars-CoV2 was a newly emerged zoonotic virus, that either jumped to humans or it was a leak from a lab. Or perhaps a reckoning from God. No one really knows. All I know, is that one day, it hit my hospital like a freight train. We had been hearing rumors about how terrible it was and how quickly patients succumbed to it but never fully understood it until we witnessed it first-hand. People underestimated it. They said it was just a flu, no big deal. It would just go away.

To say it is terrifying is an understatement. To be un-able to defeat an unseen enemy is unbearable. To know

it's airborne and is thriving is even more incompre-
hensible and terrifying. I had been in my field fourteen
years and had never, ever had to wear a PAPR hood and
or full safety gear like a biohazard astronaut until CO-
VID arrived in my home state of Arizona. No one believed it at first, everyone was in complete denial. And
when we first told people it was real, they grew angry,
almost defiant. They couldn't believe that an unseen
enemy could kill us all, crush the economy and forever
change our very existence. Yet here we are. We are now
sitting in its fourth wave, in its fifth or sixth variant
strain and we are now millions exposed. We have been
in this mighty fight almost two whole years now. It is
a living beyond heart wrenching. To see our patients
come down with COVID was only the beginning. We, in
the radiology department, just did our jobs. We X-rayed
every single one of our patients in all our COVID units.
The speed of the decline in which the patient just died
was incredible. One minute they were talking, half-jok-
ing saying hope they don't die, to one hour later going
into full blown intubation. All I could do, was wonder if
he got to say goodbye to his or her family.

To see our nation's heroes suffering daily is something I never want to experience again. Sadly though,
that is my reality. I pray for the day that COVID ends
and that we are not ever again permeated by such an
enormous tragedy. It has burned through the popula-

tion like wildfire just decimating the population. Going into the COVID units was eerily quiet. All I could ever hear was my heavy breathing, as I tried to steel my nerves and not be scared. I gave myself a pep talk every time I did an x-ray, "You can do this, through Christ all things are possible." And I did my job as best I could. It felt like it was a horror movie. Everyone behind plastic, everyone in masks and or hoods. The patients frightened, unable to see our faces to allow them to know that we genuinely cared and all we got were scared open eyes and their desperate grips through our double gloved hands. It broke my heart to see them intubated, suffering, with their family pictures on the walls and drawings from loved ones. I would be standing there in silence, just listening to my oxygen filtering behind my masks and plastic hood; wondering, hoping they would live. Watching them every day as Covid ravaged their bodies. I remember seeing a wedding picture once, the family smiling, holding hands, smiling. I just cried. I was thankful for the plastic hood then, no one could see me almost lose it. I prayed for all of them, I pray for them still. I pray God will release us from this living nightmare. I ended up catching COVID myself, and now have permanently scarred lungs and I can no longer wear protective gear, so I no longer go into the COVID units. I was unable to sleep for months, worried sick that I would bring home COVID to my family. I was so careful and yet managed to catch it. Everything and everyone are trying to normalize, whatever that means. However, the killer is still in our midst, decimating, without end. There is no end in sight. I pray we all survive yet another day. I am no longer afraid. I have the knowledge that I will live again regardless and that is enough for me. In retrospect, I do have to be grateful for some things that the pandemic has brought out. The truth of our hearts. It fully exposed the callous, the kind, the weakest societal links; where communications failed and showed our deficiencies in all areas of life. We were taking life for granted. It now made us see our greatest gift of all, the human heart and our indomitable spirit. I learned that the human spirit cannot be broken. We are still here. We are still alive and that must be enough. And I know that this too, shall pass.

CHAPTER 11

I Testify

I know now we are spirit children. That we each have a mission that was unfolded unto us when we were in heaven before coming here to unfold our spiritual path. To become better we must be brought low, so we can be brought high, back to heaven. I know the Lord has sufficient grace for us all if we would just accept it. Accept the truth that is being unfolded right before our very eyes. I pray that we all can fulfill our missions. I do not know what's in store for me or any of us, but I have found that I don't need to worry about that. I know that the Lord is in charge, and He will always provide a path in the light for me to follow. It doesn't matter what we want, we are here to do what the Lord wants us to do. To serve others. We must follow Jesus Christ example and listen to His teachings and follow them according-ly. I pray that when I stand before the Lord, that I will not cower before Him with all my shameful deeds and thoughts. That is my greatest fear. I pray I will stand there proudly. That is what I strive for every day. I pray that I am living in a manner that is acceptable to the Lord and that I am doing his work here on Earth.

I try to teach others. I pray for the sick and when I can, I put my hands on those who give me permission, that I may heal them through the power of Jesus Christ, according to their faith. I know that that is one of the gifts that I have been given and He asked me to stop wasting my gifts and so I do, to the best of my ability. I only pray that I am not wasting time and/or purpose. I am grateful that the Lord had patience and grace enough to save me. I pray we all make our way back to heaven and that we can stand before the Lord. That He will not cast us away but allow us to enter. I pray that these truths will reach everyone. I pray that our hearts and minds and souls are filled with all that is good. Thank you, Lord, for the gift of the Holy Ghost, whom is the testifier of truth, the greatest comforter, that allows me to know that He is always with us. That He will not forsake us however, we also need to do our part.

Ask for forgiveness
Baptism
Make a covenant with the Lord
Observe Sabbath
Honor commandments
Ask the Lord for guidance all the days of our lives.

Know That Jesus Christ is our savior. That He came into our world and died and resurrected and is our greatest and only mediator. He is our only way to get back into heaven. These are the things that matter. These are the things that I know to be true. I pray that we all arrive at this same truth. I pray I will be reunited with the Lord someday. I pray we will all live again. I hope I never stray. I pray to share this truth with others. Ask for yourselves if this is true. And you will know. I do humbly say these things in the name of Jesus Christ, thy Beloved Son, our Redeemer and our Resurrected Lord. Amen.

CHAPTER 12

Knowledge

"I will show you a great journey, now write!"

The sun shines for us all. Those that feel it are full of spring and laughter! Do not shun from it. The sun belongs to those who accept it. It will darken for all someday but not fully for those who have accepted our Lord, Jesus Christ as our savior and Redeemer. He came to the Earth to save us all from ourselves. He resurrected all those who accepted Him. Those that laugh like hyenas, that did not come, are still there. They are there to this very day, conceiving ways to acquire the human spirit. Plotting ways to destroy humanity. They go around, laughing and sneering at our pitfalls and choices and follies. They enjoy seeing our great demise. I will not be one of them! I choose to follow Jesus Christ! My savior! I will be like those who heeded His calling in the days of old. They too, were resurrected! He will grant us all an equal opportunity to seal our fate.

He that knows, let him share, he that hears, let him hear. He that sees, let him see. When the clouds are full of rain, they disperse without prejudice and without worry of where the rain will fall, for it covers all in its entirety. Entirely and completely. That is the word of the Lord. This is the word to the wise. Choose not to be full of folly and know that God lives! He created all things, and it is not for man to know all things but only what the Lord Jesus to let us know. I know that He created us from dust and to dust we will return, only to be resurrected again in our celestial body someday. I know that Jesus lives! I know He came to Earth to live and die for us. He came to save the evil ones from themselves and those that accepted him, He forgave. I know He is the great mediator between us and the heavenly father. I know He pleads on our behalf. He is with us all the days of our lives and we have all been given the gift of the Holy Ghost but only those who choose to hear, can. I know that our days are numbered. I know that we will be judged for a very words, thoughts, and deeds. Even our greatest whisperings are heard as a thunderous loud bolt in the ears of our Lord so careful what you say, do and think because you cannot fool the one who hears and sees all.

May the Lord have mercy on our souls and carry us into righteousness. I know that Jesus Christ died and lives for us. He wants us all to return to our heavenly father, who waits patiently, right now, for us. But know that our time will come, and we will all be held accountable for our actions. All that we have done or have failed to do. Be upright, be full of mercy, forgiveness, kindness. Learn to be quiet like Job. Read the scriptures, ask for wisdom, pray to know the truth, as I did. If you ask with a sincere heart, a broken heart, and a contrite spirit. You will not be deceived!

I was deceived for many years; this I know to be true. But when I chose to know the truth and I asked and prayed, the Lord himself, heard me and answered me. I was given another chance, a second chance and for that I am truly humbled and grateful. I know that when I was baptized, I was literally reborn. I was immersed fully under holy waters and me and my old ways died! My old heavy spirit, all the negativity I had acquired all the days of my life were left under the surface of that water and I was brought forth new. I know this and I wish the same fate for us all. I no longer live for myself. I live only for the Lord and to walk in His light. I live to do His will and not my own. Living for our own wants and needs will only lead to our destruction. I choose to never die. I choose to follow Christ. I was granted a great gift of a second chance, wisdom, and knowledge. I have been compelled to share. I know that we are here to be of service to our fellow man and to do the Lord's work. We are on his errand.

We chose to come to Earth in our premortal state, to use our free agency to choose the right, and we swore that we would. I know that because we are here. We are here and those who did not were cast out and did not receive a mortal body. They are demons, they were the ones who were cast out because that is what they chose and now their only purpose is to bring as many men as possible down to where they are. To live in misery, forever, because that is their fate and they are angry and they want us all to pay, that's it. It is that simple. We swore to follow Christ, we swore we would choose the right, we swore to get back to heavenly Father and there we decided that we would never ever be deceived. Even if we were made to forget He asked us. "Even if you were made to forget?" He asked us, "Are you sure?" We shouted in unison, "Yea Lord, we are sure! We will follow thee all the days of our lives!" He asked us, "Even if you are tempted?" We exclaimed "Yea Lord, even if we are tempted!" He asked, "Even if you were deceived?" We all sang in unison, "We will not be deceived!" He said, "Let us proceed then."

And so it was, the Earth was created, and in six days it was made possible, this great plan of salvation. And on the 7th day he rested, and He has asked us to do the same. We were given earthly mortal body to come, forget, be tempted and hopefully not be deceived. We were that sure, that certain, that not even Satan himself could ensnare us and keep us from heavenly Father. Unfortunately, that is not what happened. Most forgot. Most have chosen to forget. Most do not believe. Most have been deceived. I pray that we can all make it back, find our way back to our heavenly Father. I pray we will not be deceived. I pray we will ask for forgiveness before the Lord. I pray we will all be baptized, repent and accept Jesus Christ as our savior, whom the Lord sent to guide us back because we are so lost, so very lost, and in the dark. He knew that this would happen, like the parent that He is. He knew that we would stumble and fall like a new parent knows their child will fall when they learn to walk, and so even knowing this, we must learn how to walk therefore we must fall in order to do so. The Lord knew it, allowed it, and expects us to grow and come forth like the parent that He is. These things I know to be true. If you do not believe me, it is to your own destruction because there is only so much time that we are allotted to come, seek and know the truth and to return, and to those who do not, will fall by the wayside. But the Lord wants us back each and every one of us, no matter how many of us there are, He loves us, and He waits for us all. He will forgive those who ask for forgiveness. He will have mercy on us. He will allow us into his Kingdom but only after we have been through a trial by fire. And it is only for a little while and then he must continue with his great plan of salvation, and He will no longer wait. He will let loose the demons upon us without care.

He will allow Satan to roam freely without remorse. And then He will allow His will to occur. Jesus Christ can save us but only if we ask and before that great time comes and then it will be too late for us all. It will be too late for those who do not repent, those who forgot, those who chose to forget. Those who allowed themselves to be deceived. Those who just plain don't care. This plan must continue. I urge everyone to heed my warnings. Ask for yourself if these things are true and I promise you the Lord will answer your prayers. May the Lord guide us, may the Lord protect us. May the Lord forgive us. May the Lord fill us with his Holy Spirit, who is the discerner of truth, who helps us to know the truth of all things. We can only acquire this salvation if we follow in Jesus Christ footsteps who is our great mediator or exemplar and savior. Pray for forgiveness. Pray for mercy and wisdom. And pray most of all, to always know the truth.

CHAPTER 13

Reflection

As I look back at my life. I wonder what it all means. Why are we all put here? What is our purpose? Where do we fit in this in immense universe? As I pondered these things, I think of the one constant. Love. Love and God.

God has created the universe and we are also His divine creation. He breathed life into us, into stars, threw planets into existence and then he made- US! How could we not be moved by that? By that powerful knowledge? One would be very close minded to not think that we too, are a great creation. I know we all wonder at what it's all about, what does it all mean? We scramble about our day just trying to get by and simply survive. But that is not what God wants for us. He wants us to LIVE! Not simply, survive. To know that we are in fact, divine. That He breathed life into us. That he made us each uniquely in His image! I hope that we know we were born out of inspiration.

When life gets to be too much, we often get bogged down in all our mundane existence. However, we must see the greater, bigger picture! We must be better than that! After all, God created US! He wants us all to be happy and at peace and living our greatest life possible.

When I start to feel sad, I think that the Lord would not want to see me suffering. That is why He sent Jesus Christ, His only begotten son, to take upon Himself all the sins of the world so that we could live our greatest life and be Saved! This life is so much more than daily things that have been put in a societal box. That we have been conditioned to see and feel. We are here for only a little while. Allow for His divinity to flow through your minds, bodies and spirits. If we must endure difficulties, then so be it but I pray it's only the lesser thereof. I know that the Lord loves me. I know that He loves us all. Know He loves us even when we don't love ourselves. I know He had sufficient grace for me, to wait for me to call upon Him. I had to be brought low so that I could look up and go high with Him. I am so grateful that I carry this knowledge in my heart, body, and spirit. That He created us. That He loves us. That He has not and will never forsake us.

I pray that when you see your children, mothers, fathers, brothers, sisters, and family that you will see God's radiance shining through them with the brightness of 10,000 suns! After all, we are made of Stardust.

We are because He willed us to be. He breathed life into our nostrils, and we became. I carry that divine knowledge every day with me. The key is to simply remember that we are because He made us. I hope we don't get lost with all this Earth stuff, Earth noise and know that it is only temporary. That we will be reunited with Him someday. My wish for us all is that we remember our divinity! To love one another and him and ourselves above all things. To treat everyone with kindness, compassion, and mercy. To appreciate his love for us all that does in fact, live in all of us, whether we like it or not, it is there. It is where we are. It is who we were meant to be. It is how we are to grow. I pray to never forget my divinity. To know always, that I am a daughter of the Highest. That we are His children! I pray that we never forget the Lord has bestowed upon us His greatest gift to us all, life. That all things are possible in His name, in Jesus Christ name! I say these things humbly. Glory to the most high God, our Heavenly Father. Amen!

Afterword

Truth speaks to spirit and the truth is both felt and known. The truth is always known. The Lord fills us daily with truth. It is up to us if we will hear or acknowledge what is in fact known. He is our compass, to be complete in our divinity, we must be filled in all aspects of life with truth, without it, everything is simply an illusion. It must be who we are at the very core of our being. When we live by truth, light will shine, and darkness will naturally depart by universal law. We are divine. It is the very inheritance that our heavenly Father gave us. Let us not squander it. Let us be continuously filled with it, so much so, that it cannot help but overflow. That is who we are and that is who God created us to be and what will inevitably guide us back to him. It is up to us to choose to take it, truth and love, God's constant guidance. May the Lord bless us all and may peace be unto you. And may peace be unto us all.

Postscript

There are times in our lives when we feel we are unanchored, that even if a slight wind blew it would push and roll us over. That is the life of an unbeliever, a person who is not God centered or is not living a God centered life. A person who has not yet realized their full potential. They have not yet come to terms with their full God given divinity.

About the Author

Jeanette P. Hernandez is a Born-again Christian. Her debut book, An Everlasting Truth, is her own, very personal and spiritual journey about how she came to know God. She holds two associates degrees, one in Liberal Arts and the other in Radiologic Sciences. She is also a mother, Latter-Day Saint, United States Marine and a proud veteran. She also serves our nation's heroes, as an X-ray tech, at the Southern Arizona Veteran's Hospital in Tucson, AZ, where she currently resides.

CPSIA information can be obtained
at www.ICGtesting.com
Printed in the USA
FSHW011520120122
87605FS